AMERICA
THE BEAUTIFUL

by Katharine Lee Bates

additional text by Kristine Lombardi Frankel

Photography credits: Cover and pages 2, 3, 4, 5, 6, 7, Photodisc; page 8, Brooke Slezak, Getty Images, Inc.; page 9, © Jerry Tobias/CORBIS; pages 10, 11, Photodisc;
page 12, © CORBIS; page 13, Photodisc; page 14, © James L. Amos/CORBIS; page 15, Photodisc; page 16, © CORBIS; pages 17, 18, Photodisc; page 19, Alan Thornton, Getty Images, Inc.;
page 20, © AFP/CORBIS; page 21, © Robert Maass/CORBIS; pages 22, 23, 24, Photodisc; page 25, National Aeronautics and Space Administration;
page 26, James Balog, Getty Images, Inc.; page 27, Falmouth Historical Society and Photodisc; pages 29, 30, 31, Photodisc.

ISBN 0-8167-7490-0

Printed in the United States of America.

10 9 8 7 6 5 4 3 2 1

O beautiful for spacious skies,

For amber waves of grain,

For purple mountain majesties

Above the fruited plain!

America! America!

God shed his grace on thee

And crown thy good with brotherhood

From sea to shining sea!

O beautiful for pilgrim feet

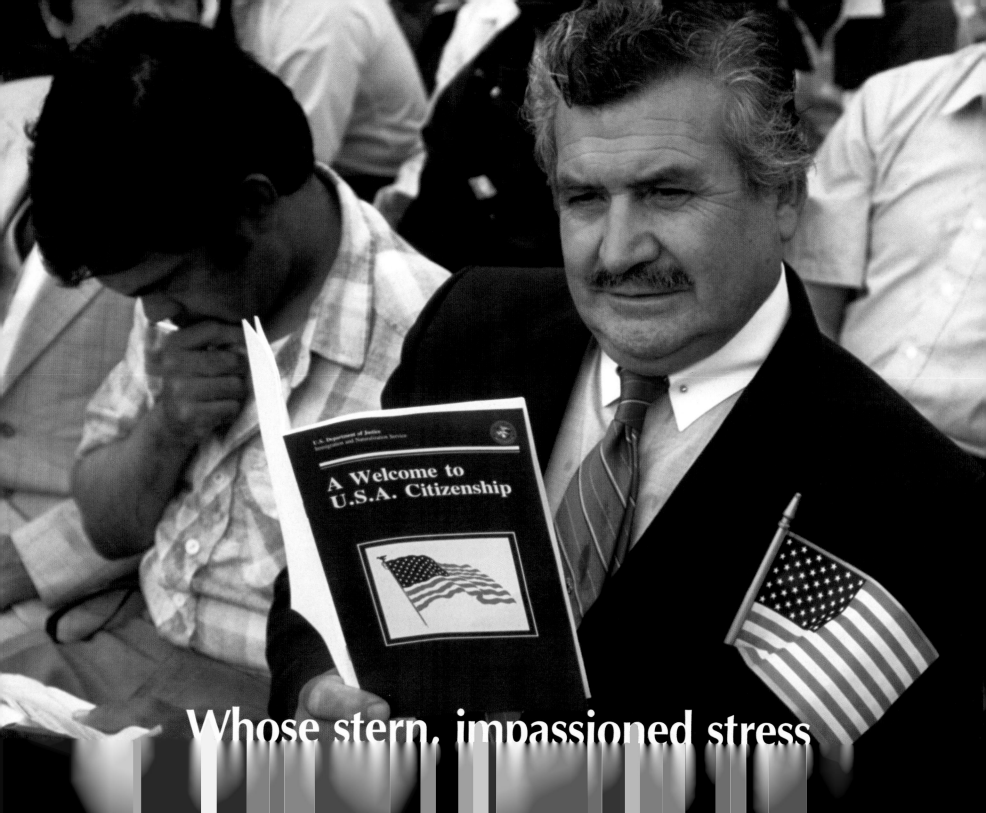

A Welcome to
U.S.A. Citizenship

U.S. Department of Justice
Immigration and Naturalization Service

Whose stern, impassioned stress

A thoroughfare for freedom beat

Across the wilderness!

America! America!

God mend thine every flaw,

Confirm thy soul in self-control,

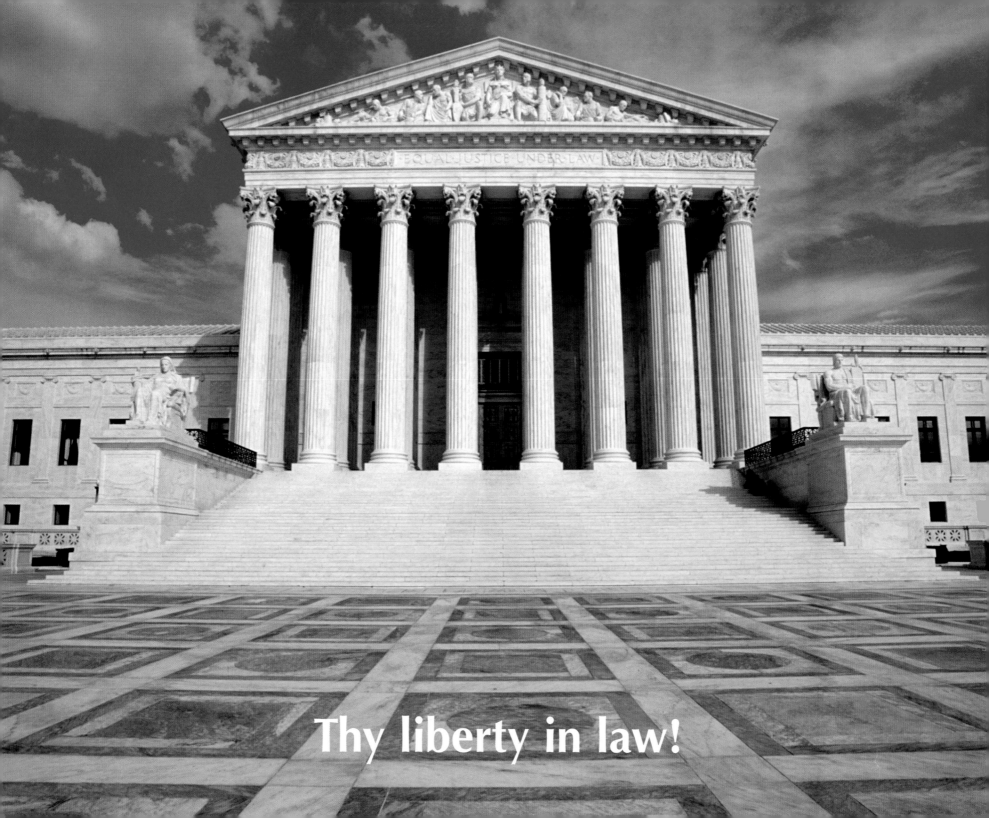

Thy liberty in law!

O beautiful for heroes proved

In liberating strife.

Who more than self the country loved

And mercy more than life!

America! America!

May God thy gold refine

Till all success be nobleness

And every gain divine!

"America the Beautiful" was written by Katharine Lee Bates in 1893. She wrote the poem after climbing Pike's Peak, a 14,000-foot mountain in Colorado.

Katharine Lee Bates

Katharine was born in 1859 and was graduated from Wellesley College in Massachusetts. She became a teacher at the college, and later she was made head of the English department. By 1893 she had written several books.

"America the Beautiful" was first published in 1895. The poem was revised several times and was published again in the *Boston Evening Transcript* in 1904. The final version of the song was written in 1913.

The poem was not intended as a song, but it fit a melody called "Materna," written by Samuel Augustus Ward in 1882.

AMERICA THE BEAUTIFUL

O beautiful for spacious skies,
For amber waves of grain,
For purple mountain majesties
Above the fruited plain!
America! America!
God shed his grace on thee
And crown thy good with brotherhood
From sea to shining sea!

O beautiful for pilgrim feet
Whose stern, impassioned stress
A thoroughfare for freedom beat
Across the wilderness!
America! America!
God mend thine every flaw,
Confirm thy soul in self-control,
Thy liberty in law!

O beautiful for heroes proved
In liberating strife.
Who more than self the country loved
And mercy more than life!
America! America!
May God thy gold refine
Till all success be nobleness
And every gain divine!

O beautiful for patriot dream
That sees beyond the years
Thine alabaster cities gleam
Undimmed by human tears!
America! America!
God shed his grace on thee
And crown thy good with brotherhood
From sea to shining sea!

O beautiful for halcyon skies,
For amber waves of grain,
For purple mountain majesties
Above the enameled plain!
America! America!
God shed his grace on thee
Till souls wax fair as earth and air
And music-hearted sea!

O beautiful for pilgrim feet,
Whose stern, impassioned stress
A thoroughfare for freedom beat
Across the wilderness!
America! America!
God shed his grace on thee
Till paths be wrought through wilds of thought
By pilgrim foot and knee!

O beautiful for glory-tale
Of liberating strife
When once and twice, for man's avail
Men lavished precious life!
America! America!
God shed his grace on thee
Till selfish gain no longer stain
The banner of the free!

O beautiful for patriot dream
That sees beyond the years
Thine alabaster cities gleam
Undimmed by human tears!
America! America!
God shed his grace on thee
Till nobler men keep once again
Thy whiter jubilee!

DID YOU KNOW...

- the American flag should be displayed only from sunrise to sunset unless there is a light shining on it?

- the flag should be displayed in or near every school?

- the flag should never touch anything beneath it, such as the ground, the floor, or water?

- when a flag has "served its useful purpose" it should be burned?

- the traditional way of folding the flag produces a triangle shape?

- the flag is flown over the White House only when the President is in Washington, D.C.?